FAST &
DELICIOUS

FAST &
DELICIOUS

hamlyn

Published in the UK in 1998
by Hamlyn, a division of Octopus Publishing Group Ltd
2–4 Heron Quays, London E14 4JP

This edition published 2002 by Octopus Publishing Group Ltd

ISBN 0 600 60825 5

Printed in China

NOTES

Both metric and imperial measurements have been given in all
recipes. Use one set of measurements only and not a
mixture of both.

Standard level spoon measurements are used in all recipes.
1 tablespoon = one 15 ml spoon
1 teaspoon = one 5 ml spoon

Eggs should be medium to large unless otherwise stated.
The Department of Health advises that eggs should not be
consumed raw. This book contains dishes made with raw or
lightly cooked eggs. It is prudent for more vulnerable people such
as pregnant and nursing mothers, invalids, the elderly, babies and
young children to avoid uncooked or lightly cooked dishes made
with eggs. Once prepared, these dishes should be kept
refrigerated and used promptly.

Milk should be full fat unless otherwise stated.

Meat and poultry should be cooked thoroughly. To test if poultry
is cooked, pierce the flesh through the thickest part with a
skewer or fork – the juices should run clear, never pink or red. Do
not re-freeze poultry that has been frozen previously and thawed.

Do not re-freeze a dish that has been frozen previously.

Pepper should be freshly ground black pepper unless
otherwise stated.

Fresh herbs should be used, unless otherwise stated. If
unavailable, use dried herbs as an alternative but halve the
quantities stated.

Measurements for canned food have been given as a standard
metric equivalent.

Nuts and nut derivatives
This book includes dishes made with nuts and nut derivatives. It
is advisable for customers with known allergic reactions to nuts
and nut derivatives and those who may be potentially vulnerable
to these allergies, such as pregnant and nursing mothers,
invalids, the elderly, babies and children, to avoid dishes made
with nuts and nut oils. It is also prudent to check the labels of
pre-prepared ingredients for the possible inclusion of nut
derivatives.

Ovens should be preheated to the specified temperature – if
using a fan-assisted oven, follow the manufacturer's
instructions for adjusting the time and the temperature.

Contents

Introduction

Today's busy lifestyles often lead us to rely more and more on packaged pre-cooked convenience meals, ready to heat through in the oven or microwave with the minimum of effort. However, there comes a time when you become tired of such ready-prepared meals. Take another look at home cooking. It can actually take far less time than you think to create tasty and imaginative meals to suit you, the family or even a few friends if you are planning an informal supper.

In *Fast & Delicious* you will find a wide collection of recipes designed to give the busy cook more time to relax. All the recipes are easy-to-prepare and, apart from a few desserts that need chilling, can be made to serve within 30 minutes. They use a variety of easily accessible ingredients: fresh produce and good-quality basic store cupboard staples. There are simple-to-prepare and delicious recipes for everyday eating, as well as informal entertaining and desserts, too, for those who crave something

sweet to complete the meal. As this book proves, quick cooking does not mean boring and unimaginative fast food. On the contrary, using a variety of ingredients and cooking methods you can produce great meals in no time at all.

QUICK COOKING IDEAS

Not only does quick cooking enable the cook to produce something good to eat within minutes, it is actually the best treatment for many fresh ingredients.

Rapid cooking is certainly the best way to keep shellfish tasting of the sea (see Mussels Provençal, page 41) and, on the same theme, there is no better way to serve baby vegetables than simply and lightly cooked, so as to retain their crispy crunchy textures and bold flavours. Grilling, pan-frying and sautéing are all useful fast cooking methods, too – try Pan-Fried Squid with Chillies on page 69 or Sautéed Beef with Mustard and Cashew Nuts on page 59. Of all the methods of cooking, however, stir-frying must certainly be one of the quickest.

STIR-FRIES

Once an exclusive oriental style of cooking, stir-frying is now an established part of everyday cuisine. Thinly sliced fresh

pasta sauces, which can be made in the time it takes for the pasta to cook (see pages 10–27 for some delicious ideas). Alternatively you can almost always find something in the store cupboard to go with pasta: simply stir into cooked pasta a spoonful from a jar of olive paste or a pesto and warm it through. Use fresh pasta, which cooks very quickly, and keep a variety of dried pasta in the cupboard as an essential stand-by.

Other useful items for your store cupboard are ready-made pizza bases. They are widely available and offer endless possibilities for toppings. Try the Vegetable Pizza on page 53 or make your own combinations, using a mixture of fresh and canned ingredients and dried herbs, for example.

vegetables, seafood, meat and poultry can all be cooked very quickly and combined with fresh spices or essential store cupboard seasonings and flavourings such as soy sauce, five-spice powder or nam pla (fish sauce). Add a packet of egg noodles or rice vermicelli from the cupboard and you have your quick meal.

Try some of the appealing stir-fries on pages 28–37 and you will soon consider the wok an indispensable item in your kitchen. For speedy cooking remember it is important to use tender ingredients and for stir-frying they should be cut into thin, even pieces, such as sticks, thin slices or shreds.

PASTA AND PIZZA

Pasta comes in all shapes and sizes and, equally, there is a huge variety of

SALADS AND DRESSINGS

Although not necessarily 'cooked', salads certainly come into the category of quick meals and have progressed far from the days of a limp round lettuce leaf, a few thick slices of cucumber and a quartered tomato on the edge of a plate. They have become whole meals in their own right and a look at many of the recipes given here will convince you of that.

The variety of fresh ingredients now on display all year round enables you to produce both traditional and more exotic salads very quickly, with tasty and nutritious results. A huge range of salad and herb leaves is now available in the shops and the supply of baby vegetables which need little or no cooking offers exciting alternatives to the traditional salad ingredients.

Salads can consist of vegetables alone or are equally enhanced by the addition of nuts and wisely chosen fresh fruit, or by seafood (see Thai Prawn Salad, page 50), meat or poultry, or cheese. This is another item of which there are now many new varieties available – sheep's and goat's cheeses are increasingly popular and Italian mozzarella goes particularly well with fresh tomatoes (see Tomato, Mozzarella and Basil Stacks, page 42).

As for salad dressings these, too, have progressed from the traditional option of ready-made salad cream. You can easily make your own creamy sauces based on fromage frais or soured cream, enhanced by herbs or other flavourings from your cupboard. Alternatively, use your store cupboard essentials to create delicious herby, garlicky, mustard or lemony vinaigrettes, or simply use a drizzling of good-quality extra virgin olive oil as a dressing.

SHORTCUTS AND ACCOMPANIMENTS

While it may be satisfying to prepare all of your ingredients yourself it is undoubtedly time consuming and these days there are many alternatives. You can often buy fresh vegetables and fruit, ready washed and sliced for instant use in stir-fries or salads. Fish is often available filleted and meat may be boned and sliced or cubed. Alternatively, you can ask the fishmonger or butcher to prepare the ingredients as you want them.

BREADS

A look in the bread section of any good grocers or supermarket will reveal the dazzling range of internationally inspired breads available. Many of these make ideal accompaniments to a quickly prepared meal, eaten just as they are or simply warmed through. Try, among others, country bread, mini baguettes, pitta bread, ciabatta, focaccia with sun-dried tomatoes or olives, plain or garlic naan bread – to go with salads, pasta dishes or curries.

PRESENTATION

Finally, a quickly prepared meal does not need to look hurriedly thrown together or unappetizing. A minute spent on presentation can make all the difference to the appearance of food. A sprig of fresh herbs or watercress, or a few cherry tomatoes scattered on top can lift a dish above the ordinary. Assorted prepared salad leaves are readily available and the mixed leaf shapes and colours not only look attractive but make a good accompaniment and a quick alternative to cooked fresh vegetables.

The good news is that quick cooking can be fun and imaginative with delightful results, and it is hoped that you will find *Fast & Delicious* just that. Go ahead and enjoy the recipes!

Pasta Dishes and Risottos

Universally popular, pasta and rice are essential convenience foods. The two combine well with an enormous variety of both fresh and canned ingredients to produce wholesome, tasty meals fast. The assorted pasta dishes and sauces and creamy risottos in this section offer plenty of choice when a quick meal is the order of the day.

Spaghetti with Tomato and Egg Sauce

Preparation time: 5 minutes, plus making the tomato sauce
Cooking time: 5 minutes, plus sauce

- 1 quantity Quick Tomato
  Sauce (see page 40)
- 2 eggs
- 25 g/1 oz Parmesan cheese,
  freshly grated
- 4 tablespoons mascarpone
  cheese or single cream
- 500 g/1 lb fresh spaghetti
- 25 g/1 oz butter
- salt and pepper
- basil leaves, to garnish

1 Make the quick tomato sauce according to the recipe on page 40 and keep warm.

2 Beat together the eggs, Parmesan and mascarpone or cream until evenly combined. Season with salt and pepper.

3 Add the spaghetti to a large saucepan of lightly salted boiling water. Return to the boil and cook over a medium heat for *3–4 minutes* until the spaghetti is *al dente*. Drain well, toss with the butter and plenty of pepper and transfer to 4 warmed serving plates.

4 Remove the tomato sauce from the heat and whisk in the egg mixture. Pour over the spaghetti and serve at once garnished with basil leaves.

Serves 4

variation _____

Farfalle with Ricotta and Tomato Sauce

Preparation time: 5 minutes, plus making the tomato sauce
Cooking time: 10 minutes, plus sauce

- 1 quantity Quick Tomato
  Sauce (see page 40)
- 300 g/10 oz dried farfalle
- 300 g/10 oz ricotta or curd
  cheese
- 1 tablespoon freshly grated
  Parmesan cheese
- salt and pepper

1 Follow step 1 of the main recipe.

2 Add the farfalle to a large saucepan of salted boiling water. Stir and bring back to the boil. Reduce the heat and boil, uncovered, for *8–10 minutes*, or according to packet instructions, stirring occasionally.

3 Put the ricotta or curd cheese in a large bowl, add the grated Parmesan and 3–4 tablespoons of the pasta cooking water. Beat the cheeses until they are creamy in consistency.

4 Drain the farfalle well. Add to the cheese and toss well to mix together. Divide the pasta equally between 4 warmed serving bowls. Taste the tomato sauce, adjust the seasoning if necessary. Pour the sauce over the pasta and serve at once.

Serves 4

Pasta with Prawns, Peas and Mint Pesto

Preparation time: 5 minutes
Cooking time: 10 minutes

- 375 g/12 oz dried tagliatelle
  or spaghetti
- 6 tablespoons walnut or
  olive oil
- 1 leek, sliced
- 2 garlic cloves, sliced
- 375 g/12 oz cooked peeled
  prawns

- 125 g/4 oz peas, thawed if
  frozen
- 4 tablespoons single cream
- 25 g/1 oz chopped walnuts,
  toasted
- salt and pepper
- sprigs of mint, to garnish

MINT PESTO:
- 3 tablespoons chopped fresh
  mint
- ½ tablespoon chopped flat
  leaf parsley
- ½ garlic clove, chopped
- ½ tablespoon freshly grated
  Parmesan cheese

- ½ tablespoon double cream
- ½ teaspoon balsamic vinegar
- 1–2 tablespoons extra virgin
  olive oil
- 3 tablespoons chopped mint
- salt and pepper

1 To make the mint pesto, place all the pesto ingredients in a food processor or blender and blend until fairly smooth. Season to taste and set aside.

2 Place the pasta in a large saucepan of salted boiling water. Return to the boil and cook for *10 minutes* or until the pasta is *al dente*.

3 Meanwhile, heat the oil in a large frying pan and stir-fry the leek and garlic for *5 minutes* until softened. Stir in the prawns and peas and heat through.

4 Drain the pasta and immediately stir in the pesto, cream and salt and pepper to taste and toss with the prawns and peas. Serve at once, topped with the walnuts and garnished with sprigs of mint.

Serves 4

Linguine with Vegetables

Preparation time: 10 minutes
Cooking time: 10 minutes

- 1 red pepper, cored,
  deseeded and cut into large
  squares
- 1 courgette, sliced
- 1 red onion, sliced
- 1 small aubergine, thinly
  sliced
- 8 asparagus spears, trimmed
- 3 tablespoons peas, cooked

- 5 tablespoons olive oil
- 300 g/10 oz linguine
- 125 g/4 oz Parmesan cheese,
  freshly grated
- handful of basil leaves,
  roughly torn
- salt and pepper

1 The fresh vegetables can be either cooked on a griddle or grilled. To griddle them, heat the griddle pan then add the peppers, skin side down, and griddle until the skin blisters and blackens. Griddle the courgette, onion and aubergine slices and the asparagus for *2 minutes* on each side. Alternatively, cook them all under a preheated hot grill.

2 Peel the skin off the pepper and slice the pepper into ribbons. Place in a dish with the courgette, onion, aubergine, asparagus, and the peas, drizzle with olive oil and place in a warm oven to keep warm.

3 Meanwhile, place the pasta in a large saucepan of salted boiling water and cook for *3–4 minutes* if fresh or *8 minutes* if dried, or according to packet instructions.

4 Drain the pasta then return it to the saucepan. Add the warm vegetables, season with salt and pepper and add the Parmesan. Toss well, using two spoons, adding a little more olive oil if necessary. Finally add the torn basil leaves and toss again, then serve immediately.

Serves 4

Lemon and Basil Orzo

Preparation time: 10 minutes
Cooking time: 10 minutes

- 2 garlic cloves, chopped
- large handful of basil leaves
- 5 tablespoons olive oil
- grated rind and juice of
  2 lemons
- 300 g/10 oz dried orzo, or

  other small dried pasta
- 150 g/5 oz Parmesan cheese,
  freshly grated
- salt and pepper
- strips of lemon rind, to
  garnish

1 Using a pestle and mortar or a food processor, blend the garlic, basil, olive oil, lemon rind and juice until smooth.

2 Place the orzo in a large saucepan of lightly salted boiling water and cook for *6–8 minutes*, or according to packet instructions.

3 Add the Parmesan to the basil mixture, season with salt and pepper and blend well.

4 Drain the orzo thoroughly. Add the basil mixture and mix well so that the sauce is distributed evenly throughout the orzo. Serve immediately, garnished with strips of lemon rind.

Serves 4

Spaghettini with Scallops and Chilli

Preparation time: 15 minutes
Cooking time: 15 minutes

- 50 ml/2 fl oz olive oil
- 125 g/4 oz fresh brown breadcrumbs
- 50 g/2 oz butter
- 500 g/1 lb fresh scallops, prepared
- 2 large red chillies, sliced
- 500 g/1 lb spaghettini
- 100 g/3½ oz pecorino cheese, grated
- small bunch of flat leaf parsley
- salt and pepper

1 Heat the oil in a heavy pan over a moderate heat. Add the breadcrumbs and cook, stirring continuously, until golden brown and crispy. Remove the crumbs and set aside. Wipe the pan with a piece of kitchen paper.

2 Heat the pan again and add the butter. Cook the scallops in small batches over a moderately high heat for *1 minute*. Add more butter if needed. Remove the scallops and set aside. Add the chillies, cook them quickly and remove.

3 Cook the spaghettini in a large pan of salted boiling water for *3–4 minutes* or according to packet instructions. Drain well. Toss with the crispy crumbs, pecorino, parsley, salt and pepper. Place in a large, warmed serving bowl and top with the scallops and chillies.

Serves 6–8

Bucatini with Rocket and Tomato

Preparation time: 15 minutes
Cooking time: 15 minutes

- 2 tablespoons olive oil
- 4 garlic cloves, finely chopped
- 90 g/3½ oz pine nuts
- 1 kg/2 lb firm ripe tomatoes, chopped
- 3 small green chillies, finely chopped
- 75 g/3 oz raisins, roughly chopped
- small bunch of rocket leaves, roughly chopped
- a few tinned anchovies, drained and finely chopped
- 500 g/1 lb bucatini pasta
- 50 g/2 oz Parmesan cheese, shaved
- 50 g/2 oz black olives, pitted
- salt and pepper

1 Heat the oil in a large heavy frying pan. Add half the garlic and all of the pine nuts. Cook, stirring often, until lightly golden. Remove from the pan and set aside.

2 Add the tomatoes, the remaining garlic and the chillies to the pan. Cook, uncovered and stirring often, over a high heat for *10 minutes* or until the mixture has reduced and thickened.

3 Stir in the raisins, rocket, reserved garlic and pine nuts. Cook for a further *1 minute*. Remove from the heat and stir in the anchovies.

4 Meanwhile, cook the bucatini pasta in a large pan of salted boiling water for *10 minutes* or according to packet instructions.

5 Drain well and toss the pasta with the tomato sauce. Season with salt and pepper to taste. Serve in warmed bowls and top with the shavings of Parmesan and the black olives.

Serves 6–8

Pasta with Crab and Lemon Sauce

Preparation time: 12 minutes
Cooking time: 7 minutes

- 1 teaspoon olive oil
- 4 garlic cloves, finely sliced
- 375 ml/13 fl oz can low-fat evaporated milk
- finely grated rind of 2 lemons
- 4 teaspoons French mustard
- 1 teaspoon cornflour
- 50 ml/2 fl oz water
- 500 g/1 lb dried angel hair pasta
- 200 g/7 oz can crabmeat
- salt and pepper

1 Heat the oil in a saucepan. Add the garlic and cook over a low heat for about *2 minutes* or until the garlic is golden. Remove the garlic from the pan and set aside.

2 Add the evaporated milk, lemon rind and French mustard to the pan. Bring slowly to the boil. Reduce the heat and simmer for about *2 minutes*.

3 Place the cornflour in a small bowl and stir in the water to form a smooth paste. Stir the cornflour paste into the milk mixture. Stir constantly over a medium heat until the mixture boils and thickens.

4 Cook the angel hair pasta in a large saucepan of salted boiling water until just tender (it will take only *1–2 minutes* since the pasta is very fine). Drain the pasta well, reserving 125 ml/4 fl oz of the cooking liquid. Toss this liquid through the pasta to help keep it moist and separate.

5 Flake the crabmeat and add it with the cooked garlic to the pasta. Transfer to warmed plates. Pour the prepared sauce over the pasta, season with black pepper and serve immediately.

Serves 6–8

Green Vegetable Risotto

Preparation time: 10 minutes
Cooking time: 20 minutes

- 1 litre/1¾ pints chicken or
  vegetable stock
- 125 g/4 oz butter
- 1 tablespoon olive oil
- 1 garlic clove, chopped
- 1 onion, finely diced
- 300 g/10 oz arborio rice
- 125 g/4 oz green beans,
  trimmed and cut into
  2.5 cm/1 inch pieces
- 125 g/4 oz peas, thawed if
  frozen
- 125 g/4 oz asparagus,
  trimmed and cut into
  2.5 cm/1 inch pieces
- 125 g/4 oz baby spinach,
  chopped
- 75 ml/3 fl oz dry vermouth or
  white wine
- 2 tablespoons chopped flat
  leaf parsley
- 125 g/4 oz Parmesan cheese,
  freshly grated
- salt and pepper

1 Place the chicken or vegetable stock in a saucepan and simmer gently.

2 Melt 50 g/2 oz of the butter with the olive oil in a heavy saucepan. Add the garlic and onion and sauté gently for *5 minutes*; do not brown.

3 Add the rice, stirring well to coat each grain with the butter and oil. Add enough stock to just cover the rice, stir again and simmer gently, stirring as frequently as possible.

4 When most of the liquid is absorbed, add more stock; keep adding stock, stirring and simmering gently until the stock is absorbed. When you add the last of the stock, add the vegetables and vermouth or white wine, mix well and cook for *2 minutes*. The risotto should have a creamy consistency.

5 Remove the pan from the heat, season with salt and pepper and add the remaining butter, the parsley and Parmesan. Mix well and serve at once.

Serves 4

Pumpkin Risotto

Preparation time: 5 minutes
Cooking time: 25 minutes
Oven temperature: 220°C (425°F), Gas Mark 7

- 1 butternut pumpkin or
  squash, weighing 1 kg/2 lb
- 3 tablespoons olive oil
- 1 litre/1¾ pints chicken or
  vegetable stock
- 125 g/4 oz butter
- 1 garlic clove, crushed
- 1 onion, finely diced

- 300 g/10 oz arborio or
  carnaroli rice
- 150 g/5 oz Parmesan cheese,
  freshly grated
- salt and pepper
- pumpkin oil, to drizzle
- Parmesan shavings, to serve

1 Top and tail the pumpkin or squash, cut in half round the middle, then pare away the skin from one half, without losing too much of the flesh. Cut in half lengthways, remove the seeds and cut into 5 cm/2 inch dice. Repeat with the other half. Place on a large baking sheet, drizzle with 2 tablespoons of the olive oil and season with salt and pepper. Mix well and cook in the top of a preheated oven, 220°C (425°F), Gas Mark 7, for *15 minutes*. The pumpkin or squash should be soft and slightly browned.

2 Meanwhile, heat the stock to a gentle simmer in a saucepan. Heat the remaining olive oil and 50 g/2 oz of the butter in a heavy saucepan, add the garlic and onion and sauté gently for *5 minutes*; do not brown.

3 Add the rice, stir well to coat the grains with oil and butter, then add enough stock to cover the rice. Stir well and simmer gently. Continue to stir as frequently as possible throughout cooking. As the liquid is absorbed, continue adding ladlefuls of stock to just cover the rice and stir well.

4 Remove the pumpkin or squash from the oven and add it to the risotto with the Parmesan and the remaining butter. Season with salt and pepper and stir gently.

5 Serve the risotto on warmed plates with the Parmesan shavings and a little pumpkin oil drizzled on top of each portion.

Serves 4

Chicken and Tomato Pasta

Preparation time: 5 minutes
Cooking time: 20 minutes

- 375 g/12 oz dried penne, conchiglie or gnocchi

SAUCE:
- 2 tablespoons olive oil
- 250 g/8 oz boneless, skinless chicken breasts, diced
- 1 large onion, finely chopped
- 3 celery sticks, diced
- 2 carrots, diced
- 2 teaspoons dried oregano
- 125 ml/4 fl oz red wine
- 425 g/14 oz can chopped tomatoes
- salt and pepper

TO GARNISH:
- 1 tablespoon oregano leaves
- Parmesan shavings

1 For the sauce, heat the oil in a pan and fry the chicken, stirring occasionally, until lightly coloured. Add the onion, celery and carrots, and cook for *5 minutes* until softened.

2 Add the oregano, wine and tomatoes, and season to taste. Bring to the boil, cover and simmer for *10 minutes*.

3 Meanwhile, cook the pasta in salted boiling water according to packet instructions or until *al dente*. Drain and toss with half the sauce. Transfer to a warmed serving dish, spoon the remaining sauce over the top of the pasta and serve immediately, garnished with oregano leaves and Parmesan shavings

Serves 4–6

variation

Ham and Tomato Pasta

Preparation time: 5 minutes
Cooking time: 20 minutes

- 375 g/12 oz dried penne, conchiglie or gnocchi

SAUCE:
- 40 g/1½ oz butter
- 1 tablespoon olive oil
- 3 garlic cloves, finely chopped
- 175 g/6 oz cooked ham, finely diced
- 425 g/14 oz can chopped tomatoes
- salt and pepper

TO GARNISH:
- 2 tablespoons chopped basil
- 125 g /4 oz pecorino or Parmesan cheese, freshly grated

1 For the sauce, heat the butter and oil in a pan over a medium heat. Add the garlic and ham and gently fry for *4–5 minutes*.

2 Add the tomatoes and salt and pepper to taste. Simmer for *10–15 minutes*, or until well blended, stirring frequently.

3 Continue from step 3 of the main recipe and serve the pasta garnished with the basil and cheese.

Serves 4–6

Fresh Ingredients

The flavour and texture of fresh ingredients can rarely be matched by frozen or canned substitutes. Always choose fresh ingredients carefully, avoiding bruised or damaged produce. Most vegetables are best stored in a cool place; the salad drawer of the refrigerator is ideal. Store mushrooms in a paper bag, rather than a plastic one since they sweat, and keep potatoes cool or they quickly go green and sprout.

Assorted salad leaves

New potatoes

Broccoli

Cherry tomatoes

Red peppers

Baby cauliflower

Broccoli comes in several varieties and is available all year round.

Cherry tomatoes are sweet, juicy and bite-sized, best used in salads and as a garnish.

Red peppers are the ripe version of the green pepper and taste sweet and mild.

Assorted salad leaves include various leaf vegetables and herbs.

Baby cauliflower, from the brassica family, is popular for its attractive size.

New potatoes are immature 'earlies' particularly suitable for steaming and boiling.

Fresh herbs are used in cooking for their flavour and as garnishes. Thyme is very fragrant, chervil has a delicate parsley-like flavour and chives have a mild onion flavour.

Baby carrots are sweeter and more tender than later crop carrots.
Oyster mushrooms are fan-shaped with a delicate texture and flavour and are best eaten raw or lightly cooked.

Mangetout are a sweet and juicy variety of pea with very tender pods, which are eaten raw or cooked.
Baby turnips can be cooked whole and the green tops used as a spring vegetable.

Baby aubergines are commonly purple with a yellowy-green flesh.
Baby savoy cabbage is another young vegetable – a type of green cabbage with attractive wrinkly leaves.

Bean sprouts are used cooked in oriental dishes or raw in salads.
Shiitake is a firm-fleshed mushroom with a rich flavour, which can be eaten raw but tastes far better cooked.

Thyme

Baby savoy cabbage

Baby aubergines

Bean sprouts

Chervil

Shiitake

Baby carrots

Baby turnips

Oyster mushrooms

Chives

Mangetout

Spinach and Lemon Risotto

Preparation time: 5 minutes
Cooking time: 20 minutes

- 1 litre/1¾ pints chicken or
  vegetable stock
- 125 g/4 oz butter
- 1 tablespoon olive oil
- 2 shallots, finely chopped
- 300 g/10 oz arborio or
  carnoroli rice

- 500 g/1 lb spinach, chopped
- grated rind and juice of
  1 lemon
- 125 g/4 oz Parmesan cheese,
  freshly grated
- salt and pepper
- grated lemon rind, to garnish

1 Heat the stock in a saucepan to a gentle simmer.

2 Heat 50 g/2 oz of the butter and the olive oil in a heavy saucepan, add the shallots and sauté for *3 minutes*.

3 Add the rice and stir well to coat the grains thoroughly with butter and oil. Add a ladleful of stock – enough to cover the rice – and stir well. Simmer gently and continue to stir as frequently as possible, adding more stock as it is absorbed.

4 Before you add the last of the stock, stir in the spinach, lemon rind and juice and season with salt and pepper. Increase the heat, stir well then add the remaining stock and butter. Allow to cook for a few minutes, then add half of the Parmesan and mix in well. Serve the risotto garnished with the remaining Parmesan and grated lemon rind.

Serves 4

Risotto with Wild Mushrooms and Sage

Preparation time: 5 minutes
Cooking time: 20 minutes

- 1 litre/1¾ pints vegetable
  stock
- 125 g/4 oz butter
- 1 tablespoon olive oil
- 1 garlic clove, crushed
- 1 onion, finely chopped
- 250 g/8 oz wild mushrooms
  (such as morels, chanterelles
  or common open
  mushrooms), halved or
  quartered

- 300 g/10 oz arborio or
  carnaroli rice
- 75 ml/3 fl oz dry white wine
- 1 tablespoon chopped fresh
  sage, plus extra to garnish
- salt and pepper
- 125 g/4 oz Parmesan cheese,
  freshly grated, to serve
- truffle oil, to drizzle
  (optional)

1 Heat the stock to a gentle simmer in a saucepan.

2 Heat half the butter with the oil in a heavy saucepan, add the garlic and onion and sauté gently for *3 minutes*; do not brown. Add the mushrooms to the pan and continue to cook gently for *2 minutes*.

3 Add the rice and mix well so that all the grains are coated in the butter and oil. Add just enough stock to cover the rice, stir well and simmer gently, stirring as frequently as possible throughout cooking. As the liquid evaporates, continue adding ladlefuls of stock to just cover the rice and stir well.

4 Finally, add the white wine, the sage and the remaining butter to the rice and stir well. Season with salt and pepper. Serve in a separate bowl with the Parmesan and truffle oil to drizzle, if liked, and garnish with chopped sage.

Serves 4

Stir-Fries

Cooked within minutes, stir-fries are always a good option for a quick meal and many ingredients are ideal for cooking in this way. Various combinations of thinly sliced fresh vegetables, king-size prawns or thin strips of meat or chicken are lightly cooked together with spices, and served alone or with noodles or rice.

Chicken Stir-Fry with Cucumber

Preparation time: 5 minutes, plus marinating
Cooking time: 10–12 minutes

- 375 g/12 oz boneless, skinless chicken breasts, cut into thin strips
- 3 tablespoons medium dry sherry
- 2 tablespoons light soy sauce
- 3 tablespoons sunflower oil
- 2.5 cm/1 inch piece of fresh root ginger, peeled and thinly sliced
- 1 small red pepper, cored, deseeded and cut into thin strips

- 12 cm/5 inch piece of cucumber, peeled, deseeded and cubed
- 4 canned water chestnuts, sliced
- 2 spring onions, cut into 2.5 cm/1 inch lengths
- 1 teaspoon cornflour
- 1 tablespoon water
- 1 teaspoon sesame oil
- 1 tablespoon sesame seeds, toasted (optional)

1 Place the chicken strips in a bowl with 1 tablespoon of the sherry and 1 tablespoon of the soy sauce, stir well, cover and leave to marinate for as long as possible.

2 Heat a wok or large frying pan over a moderate heat. Add the oil and ginger and stir-fry for *1 minute*. Increase the heat to high, add the chicken and stir-fry for *3–4 minutes*, until the chicken is just cooked. Add the pepper, cucumber, water chestnuts and spring onions and stir-fry for *3–4 minutes*. Add the remaining sherry and soy sauce, stir thoroughly and cook for *1 minute*.

3 In a cup mix the cornflour to a paste with the water. Stir the mixture into the wok or frying pan. Cook for *2 minutes* stirring all the time. Drizzle with sesame oil, and sprinkle with the sesame seeds, if using. Serve immediately.

Serves 4

Beef and Spinach Stir-Fry

Preparation time: 15 minutes
Cooking time: 15 minutes

- 2 tablespoons peanut oil
- 500 g/1 lb beef sirloin or fillet strips
- 125 g/4 oz baby spinach leaves
- 125 ml/4 fl oz chicken stock
- 5 tablespoons soy sauce
- 50 ml/2 fl oz oyster sauce
- 1 teaspoon of sesame oil
- 2 teaspoons cornflour
- 50 ml/2 fl oz water
- 1 packet dried egg noodles

1 Place a wok or a large heavy saucepan over a high heat for *2–3 minutes*. Add 1 tablespoon of the oil and swirl it around to cover the base and sides of the pan. Add half the beef strips and cook for *2 minutes* or until cooked through. Remove the beef and set aside. Repeat with the remaining oil and beef.

2 Add the spinach to the pan and cook for *30 seconds*, or until wilted. Remove the spinach and set aside. Add the chicken stock, soy and oyster sauces, and the sesame oil to the pan, and stir to combine. In a cup, mix the cornflour into a to a smooth paste with the water.

3 Pour the blended cornflour and water into the stock mixture and stir constantly over a medium heat until the mixture boils and thickens. Boil for *1 minute* further. Add the meat and spinach, and toss gently to combine. Serve with the egg noodles, cooked to packet instructions.

Serves 4

Vegetable Chow Mein

Preparation time: 10 minutes
Cooking time: 8 minutes

- 250 g/8 oz packet fine egg
  noodles
- 2 tablespoons sesame oil
- 2 carrots, cut into
  matchsticks
- 1 green pepper, cored,
  deseeded and sliced
- 3 celery sticks, thinly sliced
  on the diagonal
- 250 g/8 oz can water
  chestnuts, drained and thinly
  sliced
- 175 g/6 oz Chinese leaves,

- shredded
- 175 g/6 oz fresh spinach
  leaves, shredded
- salt and pepper
- flat leaf parsley sprigs, to
  garnish

SAUCE:

- 2 teaspoons cornflour
- 4 tablespoons cold
  vegetable stock or water
- 2 tablespoons soy sauce
- 1 tablespoon dry sherry or
  sherry vinegar

1 To make the sauce, blend the cornflour in a jug with 2 tablespoons of the stock or water, then add the remaining stock or water and the rest of the sauce ingredients. Stir well to combine.

2 Break up the noodles slightly, then cook according to packet instructions.

3 Meanwhile, heat a wok or large frying pan until hot, add the sesame oil and heat over a moderate heat until hot but not smoking.

4 Add the carrots, green pepper, celery and water chestnuts and stir-fry for *2–3 minutes*. Add the Chinese leaves and spinach and stir-fry for *1 minute*. Pour in the sauce mixture and bring to the boil over a high heat, stirring constantly until thickened and glossy. Remove from the heat.

5 Drain the cooked egg noodles and add to the vegetables. Return the pan to a high heat and toss the ingredients together until evenly combined. Add salt and pepper to taste and serve at once garnished with flat leaf parsley sprigs.

Serves 4

Paper-thin Lamb with Garlic and Spring Onions

Preparation time: 5 minutes, plus 1 hour chilling
Cooking time: 7 minutes

- 500 g/1 lb lamb neck fillet
- 2 tablespoons groundnut or vegetable oil
- 3 large garlic cloves, thinly sliced
- ½ teaspoon chilli powder, or to taste
- ½ teaspoon soft dark brown sugar
- 2 tablespoons soy sauce
- 2 tablespoons dry sherry or sherry vinegar

- 1 large bunch of spring onions, cut into 7.5 cm/3 inch lengths, then shredded lengthways
- pinch of salt

TO SERVE:

- 1 packet dried egg noodles, cooked according to packet instructions
- 2 teaspoons sesame oil
- 1 teaspoon sesame seeds
- 4 mint sprigs

1 Wrap the lamb in clingfilm and place in the freezer for about *1 hour*, or until just frozen, then cut into thin strips across the grain, discarding any fat.

2 Heat a wok or large frying pan until hot. Add the groundnut or vegetable oil and heat over a moderate heat until hot. Add the garlic and stir-fry over a gentle heat for a few seconds to flavour the oil, then add the meat and sprinkle over the chilli powder, sugar and salt.

3 Increase the heat to high and stir-fry for *4–6 minutes* until the meat is browned on all sides. Add the soy sauce and sherry or vinegar and stir-fry for *1–2 minutes*. Serve at once on a bed of spring onions and noodles, sprinkled with the sesame oil and sesame seeds. Top with mint sprigs.

Serves 4

Pepper Beef with Mangetout

Preparation time: 10 minutes, plus 1 hour chilling
Cooking time: 15 minutes

- 500 g/1 lb fillet steak
- 2 tablespoons groundnut or vegetable oil
- 1 green chilli, finely chopped, seeds discarded according to taste
- 2.5 cm/1 inch piece of fresh root ginger, peeled and finely chopped
- 4 spring onions, finely chopped

- 1 large red pepper, cored, deseeded and diced
- 250 g/8 oz mangetout, trimmed
- 1 tablespoon Szechuan pepper or Chinese 5-spice mix
- 1 tablespoon cornflour
- 4 tablespoons soy sauce
- 2 tablespoons soft dark brown sugar
- parsley sprig, to garnish

1 Wrap the steak and place in the freezer for about *1 hour*, or until just frozen, then cut into thin slices across the grain.

2 Heat a wok or large frying pan until hot. Add 1 tablespoon of the oil and heat over a moderate heat until hot. Add the chilli, ginger, spring onions and red pepper and stir-fry over a gentle heat for *5 minutes* until well softened. Add the mangetout, increase the heat to high and stir-fry for *2 minutes*.

3 Remove all the vegetables with a slotted spoon and set aside on a plate. Wipe the pan with kitchen paper.

4 Add the Szechuan pepper to the pan and dry-fry over a gentle heat for *1–2 minutes*. Transfer to a mortar and crush with a pestle or the end of a wooden rolling pin.

5 Heat the remaining oil in the pan, add the meat and crushed pepper and increase the heat to high. Stir-fry for *2 minutes* or until the meat is browned on all sides. Remove with a slotted spoon and set aside with the vegetables.

6 Blend the cornflour in a measuring jug with 2 tablespoons of water, then add a further 2 tablespoons of water, the soy sauce and sugar. Stir well to combine and make up to 300 ml/½ pint with boiling water. Pour into the pan and bring to the boil over a high heat, stirring constantly until thickened and glossy. Return all the ingredients to the pan and stir-fry for about *1 minute* or until heated through. Serve at once garnished with parsley.

Serves 4

Hot Prawns

Preparation time: 5 minutes
Cooking time: 10 minutes

- 2 tablespoons groundnut or vegetable oil
- ½ onion, thinly sliced
- 2.5 cm/1 inch piece of fresh root ginger, peeled and thinly sliced
- 1–2 garlic cloves, thinly sliced
- 500 g/1 lb large cooked peeled prawns
- 1½ tablespoons chilli powder, or to taste
- ½ teaspoon salt
- 6 ripe tomatoes, skinned and cut into eight
- coriander sprigs, to garnish

1 Heat a wok or large frying pan until hot. Add 1 tablespoon of the oil and heat over a moderate heat until hot. Add the sliced onion, ginger and garlic to the pan and stir-fry over a gentle heat for *2–3 minutes* to blend the flavours without browning the ingredients.

2 Add the prawns, chilli powder and salt. Increase the heat to high and stir-fry for *1–2 minutes*. Tip all the ingredients out of the pan into a bowl, cover and set aside.

3 Heat the remaining oil in the pan over a moderate heat until hot. Add the tomatoes and stir-fry for several minutes until the juices run. Return the prawn mixture to the pan and stir-fry over a high heat for about *30 seconds* until heated through. Serve hot, garnished with coriander sprigs.

Serves 4

Baby Vegetable Stir-Fry with Orange and Oyster Sauce

Preparation time: 5 minutes
Cooking time: 12 minutes

- 2 tablespoons olive or
  walnut oil
- 175 g/6 oz baby carrots
- 175 g/6 oz baby corn cobs
- 175 g/6 oz small button
  mushrooms
- salt and pepper
- flat leaf parsley sprigs, to
  garnish

SAUCE:
- 2 teaspoons cornflour
- finely grated rind and juice
  of 1 large orange
- 2 tablespoons oyster sauce
- 1 tablespoon dry sherry or
  sherry vinegar

1 To make the sauce, blend the cornflour in a jug with 4 tablespoons of water, then add the orange rind and juice, oyster sauce and sherry or vinegar. Stir well to combine.

2 Heat a wok or large frying pan until hot. Add the oil and heat over a moderate heat until hot but not smoking. Add the carrots and corn cobs and stir-fry for *5 minutes*, then add the mushrooms and stir-fry for *3–4 minutes*.

3 Pour in the sauce mixture and bring to the boil over a high heat, stirring constantly until thickened and glossy. Season with salt and pepper to taste, garnish with sprigs of flat leaf parsley and serve at once.

Serves 4–6

Stir-fried Ginger with Crab

Preparation time: 10 minutes
Cooking time: 6–7 minutes

- 250 g/8 oz fresh or dried
  tagliatelle
- 1 tablespoon sesame oil
- 175 g/6 oz broccoli, broken
  into florets, stalks sliced
- 3 tablespoons vegetable oil
- 5 cm/2 inch piece of fresh
  root ginger, peeled and finely
  sliced
- 2 garlic cloves, crushed

- 4 spring onions, cut into strips
- 375 g/12 oz white crab meat,
  flaked
- salt and pepper
- soy sauce, to serve

SAUCE:
- 150 ml/¼ pint fish stock
- 4 tablespoons soy sauce
- 2 tablespoons dry sherry or
  white wine

1 Cook the tagliatelle in salted boiling water, according to packet instructions. Drain thoroughly, place in a bowl and toss with the sesame oil. Cover and keep warm.

2 Blanch the broccoli in salted boiling water for *1½ minutes*. Drain, rinse immediately under cold water and drain again.

3 To make the sauce, mix the fish stock in a jug with the soy sauce and sherry or wine. Set aside.

4 Heat a wok or large frying pan until hot. Add the vegetable oil and heat over a moderate heat until hot. Add the ginger, garlic and spring onions and stir-fry for *30 seconds* to flavour the oil; do not let them brown. Add the broccoli, increase the heat to high and stir-fry for *3–4 minutes*. Add the sauce and tagliatelle and toss until evenly mixed. Add the crab meat and toss until piping hot. Season with pepper to taste and serve at once with soy sauce handed separately.

Serves 3–4

Suppers and Snacks

Light meals often need to be produced in a hurry. This does not mean that you have to compromise on flavour, however. Despite being quickly prepared, the recipes on the following pages are deliciously tasty. Many include chicken and seafood, which are among the quickest foods to cook, and range from recipes suitable for a lunchtime snack to those for a filling, easy-to-prepare simple family supper.

Tuna Hash Patties

Preparation time: 10 minutes, plus making the tomato sauce
Cooking time: 10 minutes, plus sauce

QUICK TOMATO SAUCE:

- 425 g/14 oz jar passata
- 1 garlic clove, crushed
- 2 tablespoons olive oil
- ¼ teaspoon sugar
- 1 bay leaf
- 1 tablespoon chopped basil

PATTIES:

- 25 g/1 oz butter
- 1 small onion, chopped
- 2 garlic cloves, crushed
- 1 tablespoon chopped thyme
- 375 g/12 oz peeled potatoes, boiled, mashed and allowed to dry out
- 2 x 200 g/7 oz cans tuna in brine, drained and flaked
- 50 g/2 oz Gruyère cheese, grated
- 2 tablespoons chopped flat leaf parsley
- 1 egg, beaten
- 4 tablespoons seasoned flour
- vegetable oil, for frying
- salt and pepper

1 To make the Quick Tomato Sauce, place all the ingredients in a saucepan and bring to the boil. Cover and simmer for *10 minutes*. Taste and adjust the seasoning if necessary, discard the bay leaf and keep the sauce warm.

2 Melt the butter in a frying pan and fry the onion, garlic and thyme for *5 minutes* until softened, stir into the mashed potato and allow to cool slightly. Add the tuna, Gruyère, parsley and egg, then season with salt and pepper.

3 Divide the mixture into 8 and shape each one into a small flat patty. Dip each patty into the seasoned flour and coat well. Heat enough oil to cover the base of a large, nonstick frying pan and fry the patties in batches for *2–3 minutes* on each side until golden and crisp on the outside and heated through. Drain on absorbent kitchen paper and serve hot with the tomato sauce.

Serves 4

Provençal Mussels

Preparation time: 10 minutes
Cooking time: 15–20 minutes

- 425 g/14 oz can chopped
  tomatoes
- 1 garlic clove, chopped
- 2 tablespoons olive oil
- pinch of sugar
- 2 tablespoons chopped basil
- 6 tablespoons dry white wine
- 1 small onion, finely chopped
- 1 celery stick, chopped

- 2 tablespoons chopped
  celery leaves
- 1 tablespoon chopped flat
  leaf parsley
- 1.75 kg/3½ lb fresh mussels,
  scrubbed, debearded and
  dried
- salt and pepper
- French bread, to serve

1 Place the tomatoes, garlic, olive oil and sugar in a small saucepan, bring to the boil and simmer gently for *15 minutes*; stir in the basil.

2 Put all the remaining ingredients in a large saucepan and bring to the boil. Add the mussels, cover and steam for *5 minutes* until all the shells have opened. Discard any mussels that remain closed.

3 Transfer the mussels to a large warmed bowl with a slotted spoon, cover and set aside. Strain the cooking liquid through a fine sieve into the tomato sauce, season to taste, stir, and carefully pour over the mussels. Serve at once with plenty of French bread.

Serves 2–4

Tomato, Mozzarella and Basil Stacks

Preparation time: 10 minutes

- 4 large, firm ripe tomatoes
- 4 mozzarella balls, sliced
- handful of basil leaves
- 50 g/2 oz large black olives,
  pitted and sliced
- 2 tablespoons white vinegar
  or balsamic vinegar
- 50 ml/2 fl oz olive oil
- salt and pepper

1 Cut each tomato into 2 or 3 thick slices. Place the largest slice of each tomato on a plate, and top with a slice of mozzarella and a basil leaf. Top with another layer of tomato, mozzarella and basil.

2 Complete each stack with some sliced olives. Combine the vinegar and olive oil and season with salt and pepper. Spoon over the stacks and serve immediately.

Serves 4

Salade Niçoise

Preparation time: 10 minutes, plus marinating   Cooking time: 30 minutes

- 250 g/ 8 oz new potatoes
- 200 g/7 oz can tuna in brine, drained and flaked
- 125 ml/4 fl olive oil
- 1 tablespoon balsamic vinegar
- 1 garlic clove, crushed
- 2 tablespoons capers, drained, washed and chopped
- 2 tablespoons chopped basil
- 1 teaspoon wholegrain mustard
- 4 small eggs
- 175 g/6 oz French beans
- 500 g/1 lb ripe tomatoes, quartered
- 175 g/6 oz cucumber, sliced
- 50 g/2 oz pitted black olives
- 50 g/2 oz can anchovies in oil, drained
- salt and pepper

1 Cook the potatoes in a saucepan of lightly salted boiling water for *10–12 minutes* until just tender. Drain well, rinse briefly with cold water to stop the cooking process and place in a large bowl.

2 Add the tuna to the potatoes. Whisk together the oil, vinegar, garlic, capers, basil, mustard and salt and pepper, to taste. Pour over the tuna and potatoes, cover and leave to marinate.

3 Bring a saucepan of water to the boil, carefully spoon in the eggs and, timing from when the water returns to the boil, cook the eggs for *6 minutes* for a soft yolk or *8 minutes* for a hard yolk – as you prefer. Immediately plunge the eggs into cold water, allow to cool and then remove their shells.

4 Blanch the French beans in a pan of lightly salted boiling water for *2 minutes*. Drain the beans, refresh under cold running water and pat dry with absorbent kitchen paper.

5 Just before serving, place the tomatoes in a large bowl and add the French beans and cucumber. Carefully stir in the potatoes, tuna and all the dressing and transfer to a serving bowl. Divide the eggs into quarters and arrange them over the salad as a garnish together with the olives and the anchovies.

Serves 4

Lime Trout Pâté with Parmesan Toast

Preparation time: 15 minutes
Cooking time: 3–4 minutes
Oven temperature: 200°C (400°F), Gas Mark 6

- 2 smoked trout, skinned and
  filleted
- 500 g/1 lb soft cream cheese
- 125 ml/4 fl oz single cream
- grated rind and juice of
  2 limes
- pepper

PARMESAN TOAST:
- 1 French stick, thinly sliced
  on the diagonal
- grated Parmesan cheese, to
  sprinkle

1 Place the trout in a mixing bowl and break up with a fork, removing any fine bones.

2 Place the cream cheese and cream in a bowl. Using an electric whisk, beat for *1–2 minutes* until smooth.

3 Add the cream cheese mixture, lime rind and juice and a little pepper to the trout, and mix with a metal spoon until just combined. Spoon the mixture into pots and chill until ready to serve with the Parmesan toast.

4 To make the Parmesan toast, place the slices of French bread on a lightly oiled baking sheet, and sprinkle generously with grated Parmesan. Bake in a preheated oven, 200°C (400°F), Gas Mark 6, for *3–4 minutes*, or until the bread is crisp and golden brown.

Serves 4–6

Smoked Salmon Salad

Preparation time: 20 minutes

- **300 g/10 oz smoked salmon slices**
- **2 avocados, pitted, peeled and sliced**
- **baby curly endive leaves**
- **325 g/11 oz jar pickled and spiced asparagus or fresh, cooked asparagus**
- **100 g/3½ oz jar capers**

- **1 small onion, finely sliced into rings**
- **4 tablespoons soured cream**
- **pepper**

TO SERVE:
- **1 French stick**
- **2 limes or lemons, cut into wedges**

1 Arrange the slices of smoked salmon and avocado and the endive on individual plates. Top each serving with some asparagus, capers and onion rings.

2 Place a tablespoon of soured cream on each serving and grind black pepper over the salad. Serve the salad with some lime or lemon wedges and slices of French bread.

Serves 6

Chicken and Avocado Salad

Smoked or Tandoori chicken may be used if preferred.

Preparation time: 5 minutes

- 8 oz boneless, skinless cooked chicken, shredded
- 1 small red onion, thinly sliced
- 1 small red apple, thinly sliced
- 1 oz walnuts, roughly chopped
- 1 tablespoon sultanas
- 2 avocados, peeled, pitted and sliced

DRESSING:
- 1 teaspoon French mustard
- 3 tablespoons olive oil
- 1 tablespoon white wine vinegar
- 1 teaspoon caster sugar
- 1 garlic clove, crushed
- 1 teaspoon chopped thyme

TO SERVE:
- 1 bag of mixed salad leaves
- 1 tablespoon chopped dill

1 Place the chicken in a mixing bowl with the onion, apple, walnuts and sultanas.

2 Add the sliced avocados to the chicken mixture.

3 Mix the dressing ingredients together, pour over the chicken and avocado mixture and stir well. Place the salad leaves on four plates and top with the chicken and avocado mixture. Serve sprinkled with chopped dill.

Serves 4

variations

Salmon and Avocado

Preparation time: 10 minutes

- 250 g/8 oz cold poached salmon or drained, canned salmon
- 2 sliced avocados, peeled, pitted and sliced
- 300 ml/½ pint soured cream
- 1 teaspoon lemon juice
- 2 teaspoons chopped fresh or ½ teaspoon dried thyme
- salt and pepper
- 1 bag of mixed salad leaves, to serve

1 Remove the skin from the salmon. Flake the flesh, removing any bones, and place in a mixing bowl.

2 Carefully stir in the remaining ingredients, taking care not to break up the salmon flesh too much.

3 Serve with mixed salad leaves.

Serves 4

Tuna, Avocado and Onion

Preparation time: 5 minutes

- 200 g/7 oz can tuna, drained
- 2 sliced avocados, peeled, pitted and sliced
- 6 tablespoons mayonnaise
- 6 spring onions, chopped
- finely grated rind of 1 lemon
- salt and pepper
- 1 bag of mixed salad leaves, to serve

1 Combine the tuna, avocados, mayonnaise, spring onions and grated lemon rind in a mixing bowl. Season to taste.

2 Serve with mixed salad leaves.

Serves 4

Barbecued Chicken and Prawn Kebabs

Preparation time: 5–10 minutes
Cooking time: 20 minutes

- 750 g/1½ lb boneless, skinless chicken breasts, cut into 2.5 cm/1 inch cubes
- 20 cooked Mediterranean or large prawns, defrosted if frozen
- 1 small yellow or red pepper, cored, deseeded and cut into 2.5 cm/1 inch cubes
- 1 small green pepper, cored, deseeded and cut into 2.5 cm/1 inch cubes

HERB BASTING SAUCE:

- 4 tablespoons sunflower oil
- 2 tablespoons lemon juice
- 1 teaspoon chopped marjoram
- 1 teaspoon chopped thyme
- 2 tablespoons chopped flat leaf parsley
- 1 garlic clove, crushed
- 1 onion, finely chopped
- salt and pepper

1 To make the sauce, mix all the ingredients together in a bowl with salt and pepper to taste, or place in a screw-top jar and shake well.

2 Thread the pieces of chicken, prawns and peppers alternately on to pre-soaked bamboo or oiled metal skewers. Place the skewers in a shallow dish and pour the sauce over them. Turn the skewers to coat thoroughly.

3 Remove the kebabs from the sauce, reserving the remainder. Cook the kebabs on the oiled grill of a barbecue, or under a preheated hot grill for *20 minutes*, turning and basting frequently with the reserved sauce. Serve hot.

Serves 6–8

Caesar Salad

Preparation time: 20 minutes
Cooking time: 5 minutes

- 1 garlic clove, crushed
- 4 anchovy fillets, chopped
- 4 tablespoons lemon juice
- 2 teaspoons mustard powder
- 1 egg yolk
- 200 ml/7 fl oz extra virgin
  olive oil
- vegetable oil, for frying

- 3 slices of country bread,
  cubed
- 1 Cos lettuce, torn into
  pieces
- 3 tablespoons freshly grated
  Parmesan cheese
- pepper

1 Place the garlic, anchovy fillets, lemon juice, mustard powder and egg yolk in a small mixing bowl and season with pepper. With a hand-held blender or small whisk, mix well until combined. Slowly drizzle in the olive oil, mixing all the time to form a creamy sauce. If the sauce is too thick, add a little water.

2 Heat the vegetable oil in a frying pan. Test with a small piece of bread to see if it is hot enough: if the bread sizzles add the cubes of bread, turning them when they are golden. When they are cooked, transfer the croûtons to a plate lined with kitchen paper to absorb the excess oil.

3 Put the lettuce into a large bowl, pour over the dressing and 2 tablespoons of the Parmesan; mix well.

4 Serve the salad in a large bowl or on individual plates, sprinkle with the croûtons, the remaining Parmesan and pepper.

Serves 4

Thai Prawn Salad

Preparation time: 15 minutes

- 300 g/10 oz uncooked prawns, peeled and deveined
- 4 tablespoons water
- 200 g/7 oz onions, finely sliced
- 5 small Thai chillies, sliced, or ½ teaspoon ground chilli
- 3 tablespoons finely chopped basil or mint leaves
- 3 tablespoons chopped

- lemon grass
- 3 tablespoons lemon juice
- 3 tablespoons fish sauce (nam pla)
- ½ teaspoon sugar
- 1 Cos lettuce, separated into leaves, to serve
- 1 tablespoon chopped fresh coriander, to garnish

1 Place the prawns in a large, shallow saucepan with the measured water and cook over a moderate heat until the prawns turn pink. Do not let the water boil or the prawns will become tough.

2 Meanwhile, combine the onions, chillies or ground chilli, basil or mint, lemon grass, lemon juice, fish sauce and sugar in a bowl and mix well. Using a slotted spoon, transfer the prawns to the bowl and stir very gently, to mix.

3 Arrange a bed of lettuce on a serving plate. Top with the prawn mixture, garnish with coriander and serve.

Serves 4

variation
Thai Squid Salad

Preparation time: 15 minutes

- 300 g/10 oz prepared squid, cleaned and sliced
- 1 red onion, quartered and sliced
- 3 Thai chillies, finely chopped or 1 teaspoon ground chilli
- 3 mint sprigs, chopped
- 1½ tablespoons lemon juice
- 1 tablespoon fish sauce (nam pla)
- ½ teaspoon sugar
- coriander sprigs, to garnish

1 Place the prepared squid in a nonstick saucepan and cook, stirring constantly, for *2–3 minutes*. Remove from the heat and allow to cool.

2 Using a slotted spoon, transfer the squid to a bowl and stir in the onion, chillies or ground chilli, mint, lemon juice, fish sauce and sugar.

3 Transfer to a serving bowl and garnish with a sprig of coriander.

Serves 4

Tomato and Green Bean Salad

Preparation time: 10 minutes
Cooking time: 2 minutes

- 250 g/8 oz mixed red and
  yellow baby tomatoes, plum
  if possible
- 250 g/8 oz French beans,
  topped and tailed
- handful of chopped mint

- 1 garlic clove, chopped
- 4 tablespoons extra virgin
  olive oil
- 1 tablespoon balsamic
  vinegar
- salt and pepper

1 Cut the baby tomatoes in half and place in a large bowl.

2 Place the beans in a large saucepan of boiling water and
cook for *2 minutes*, then drain well and place in the bowl with
the tomatoes.

3 Add the chopped mint, garlic, olive oil and balsamic
vinegar. Season with salt and pepper and mix well. Serve
warm or cold.

Serves 4

Fresh Vegetable Pizza

Preparation time: 15 minutes
Cooking time: 10 minutes
Oven temperature: 230°C (450°F), Gas Mark 8

- 4 small ready-made pizza bases
- 5 tablespoons olive oil
- 2 garlic cloves, crushed
- 1 red onion, finely sliced
- 1 red pepper, cored, deseeded and cut into thin strips
- 1 yellow pepper, cored deseeded and cut into thin strips
- 4 plum tomatoes, skinned, cored and cut into wedges
- 2 courgettes, thinly sliced lengthways
- 500 g/1 lb asparagus, trimmed
- 250 g/½ lb wild mushrooms
- 4 thyme, sprigs separated into leaves
- handful of basil leaves, roughly torn
- salt and pepper

1 Place the pizza bases on warmed baking sheets, brush with a little olive oil, then arrange the vegetables on the bases, sprinkling them with the thyme leaves and roughly torn basil.

2 Season the pizzas generously with salt and pepper, drizzle with olive oil and bake at the top of a preheated oven, 230°C (450°F), Gas Mark 8, for *10 minutes*. (The vegetables should be slightly charred around the edges as this adds to the flavour.) Serve topped with fresh Parmesan shavings, if liked.

Serves 4

Pasta Bake with Spinach and Ham

Preparation time: 15 minutes
Cooking time: 15 minutes
Oven temperature: 200°C (400°F), Gas Mark 6

- 2 tablespoons olive oil
- 1 onion, chopped
- 1 garlic clove, chopped
- 750 g/1½ lb spinach, chopped
- nutmeg, freshly grated
- 8 sheets fresh spinach
  lasagne
- 250 g/8 oz ham, chopped
  into large chunks
- 125 g/4 oz packet mozzarella
  cheese, thinly sliced
- 125 g/4 oz fontina cheese,
  grated
- salt and pepper

1 Heat the olive oil in a saucepan, add the onion and garlic and sauté for *3 minutes*.

2 Add the spinach and mix well; cook for *2 minutes* over a moderate heat until the spinach starts to wilt. Add nutmeg to taste, and season with salt and pepper.

3 Lightly oil a large shallow baking dish. Place a layer of lasagne at the bottom of the dish, followed by a layer of spinach, then ham and then a layer of mozzarella. Repeat until all the ingredients are used, finishing with lasagne and the grated fontina.

4 Place the dish at the top of a preheated oven, 200°C (400°F), Gas Mark 6, and bake for *15 minutes* until golden brown and bubbling.

Serves 4

Chicken with Dolcelatte and Mascarpone Polenta

Preparation time: 5 minutes
Cooking time: 20–25 minutes

- 4 chicken breasts
- 600 ml/1 pint water
- 150 g/5 oz quick-cooking polenta flour
- 50 g/2 oz butter
- 2 tablespoons olive oil
- 75 g/3 oz dolcelatte or a similar creamy blue cheese
- 75 g/3 oz mascarpone
- handful of oregano chopped, extra to garnish
- salt and pepper

1 Place the chicken breasts under a preheated hot grill for *8–10 minutes* on each side or until cooked through, turning once. Keep warm.

2 Meanwhile, heat the water to a gentle simmer, pour in the polenta and beat well for *1–2 minutes* until it becomes a smooth paste.

3 Turn the heat down and continue to cook the polenta until it thickens, stirring constantly so that it does not catch on the bottom of the pan or form a skin on the top – it needs to cook in this way for *6–8 minutes*.

4 When the polenta is thick and cooked, season with salt and pepper, add the butter and olive oil and mix well. Break the dolcelatte into small pieces and add it to the polenta with the mascarpone and chopped oregano. Mix well.

5 The polenta should now be the consistency of soft mashed potatoes. Serve with the grilled chicken breasts. Season with salt and pepper to taste and garnish with chopped oregano.

Serves 4

Informal Entertaining

This tempting selection of recipes easily proves that entertaining does not necessarily mean complicated and time-consuming cooking. Created with appealing ingredients, the dishes here are out of the ordinary, yet can all be created in under 30 minutes, allowing you plenty of time to relax with your guests.

Steak with Fresh Tomato Sauce

Preparation time: 5 minutes
Cooking time: 20–25 minutes

- 4 rump steaks, 2 cm/¾ inch
  thick
- olive oil, for sprinkling and
  frying
- 125 ml/4 fl oz dry red wine
- salt and pepper
- basil sprigs, to garnish

SAUCE:
- 2 tablespoons olive oil
- 3 garlic cloves, crushed
- 500 g/1 lb plum tomatoes,
  skinned, deseeded and
  chopped
- a few basil leaves or
  ½ teaspoon dried oregano

1 Beat the steaks with a rolling pin to tenderize. Season with salt and pepper, sprinkle with oil and leave to stand.

2 For the sauce, heat the oil in a saucepan and sauté the garlic for *1 minute*. Add the tomatoes and season to taste with salt and pepper. Bring to the boil then cook over a moderate heat for *5 minutes*, until the tomatoes are just softened. Add the basil or oregano.

3 Oil the base of a large frying pan and sauté the steaks over a moderate heat for *2 minutes* each side, until lightly browned. Add the red wine. Top each steak with a thick layer of the sauce, cover the pan tightly and cook over a low heat for *6–10* minutes or until the steaks are tender and cooked to your liking. Serve at once on a bed of sautéed potato wedges. Garnish with a sprig of basil.

Serves 4

Sautéed Beef with Mustard and Cashew Nuts

Preparation time: 5–10 minutes
Cooking time: 10 minutes

- 6 slices of wholemeal bread
- 2 tablespoons sunflower oil
- 50 g/2 oz unsalted cashew nuts
- 6 beef fillet steaks (approximately 125–150 g/ 4–5 oz each), trimmed
- 1 tablespoon Dijon mustard
- 1 tablespoon English mustard
- 1 tablespoon coarse grain mustard (such as Meaux)
- 50 ml/2 fl oz red wine
- 125 ml/4 fl oz beef stock made from a cube
- salt and pepper

1 To make the croûtons use a biscuit cutter and cut the slices of bread into fancy shapes. Brush them with a little of the oil and toast under a hot grill until they are golden, turning them once. Set aside.

2 Toast the cashew nuts on a baking sheet under the hot grill until golden, turning them occasionally. Set aside.

3 Heat the remaining oil in a large frying pan and fry the steaks quickly for *1 minute* on each side to seal them. Pour off any excess fat. Mix together the mustards, wine and stock and pour over the beef. Simmer, uncovered, for about *5 minutes*, or until the steaks are cooked to your liking.

4 Stir in the cashew nuts. Season to taste with salt and pepper. To serve, place each steak on an individual plate and spoon over the juices and nuts. Garnish with a croûton. Serve immediately, with mangetout, if liked.

Serves 6

Salade Tiède with Calves' Liver

Preparation time: 5 minutes
Cooking time: 5 minutes

An elegant salad which needs to be served
as soon as it is assembled. The salad leaves
can be varied according to availability. If preferred,
you could buy a bag of prepared assorted leaves.

- 175 g/6 oz French beans,
  topped and tailed
- 4 tablespoons olive oil
- 250 g/8 oz calves' liver, cut
  into fine strips
- 2 spring onions, sliced
- 3 tablespoons lemon juice
- salt and pepper

- marjoram sprigs, to garnish

SALAD LEAVES:
- 3 large feuille de chêne
  leaves
- 2 large frisée or escarole
  leaves
- 4 large radicchio leaves

1 Tear up the salad leaves and arrange them on 4 serving
plates. Blanch the French beans in salted boiling water for
3–4 minutes, then scatter them on top of the lettuce.

2 Heat the olive oil in a large pan. Fry the strips of liver and
spring onions for about *2 minutes* over a fairly high heat,
turning them frequently until they are evenly coloured, but
leaving the liver slightly pink in the middle. Stir in the lemon
juice and season with salt and pepper to taste.

3 Spoon the liver mixture over the salad leaves and garnish
with the marjoram sprigs. Serve immediately.

Serves 4

variation _____

... with Chicken Livers and Grapes

Preparation time: 5 minutes
Cooking time: 5 minutes

- 50 g/2 oz butter
- 1 tablespoon sunflower oil
- 500 g/1 lb chicken livers,
  halved
- 1 teaspoon wholegrain
  mustard
- 2 tablespoons Marsala or
  medium dry sherry
- 2 teaspoons white wine
  vinegar

- 250 g/8 oz seedless white
  grapes
- assorted salad leaves,
  prepared as in the main
  recipe
- salt and pepper
- 2 tablespoons chopped flat
  leaf parsley, to garnish

1 Heat the butter and sunflower oil in a frying pan. Add the
chicken livers and fry gently until they are cooked but still pink,
about *3 minutes*.

2 Add the wholegrain mustard, Marsala or sherry and
vinegar, blending well. Stir in the grapes with salt and pepper
to taste and toss gently until hot.

3 Spoon the liver mixture over the salad leaves and garnish
with flat leaf parsley.

Serves 4

Chicken Sautéed with Mushrooms

Preparation time: 5 minutes
Cooking time: 20 minutes

The large cap field mushrooms are ideal for this recipe but any variety or mixture of varieties can be used.

- 2 tablespoons sunflower oil
- 8 small chicken portions (such as thighs and drumsticks)
- 25 g/1 oz butter
- 2 large garlic cloves, crushed
- 1 small onion, finely chopped
- 175 g/6 oz mushrooms, sliced
- 2 tablespoons dried breadcrumbs
- 2 tablespoons chopped flat leaf parsley
- salt and pepper

TO SERVE:

- 2 red peppers, thinly sliced
- 2 yellow peppers, thinly sliced
- 3 tablespoons vinaigrette dressing

1 Heat the oil in a wide saucepan or frying pan. Add the chicken portions and brown on all sides. Season with a little salt and plenty of pepper. Lower the heat and continue to cook for about *8 minutes*, stirring frequently, until the chicken is tender. Remove with a slotted spoon and set aside.

2 Increase the heat and add the butter. As soon as it has melted, add the garlic, onion and mushrooms and stir-fry over a high heat until the mushrooms are just cooked, about *4 minutes*. Stir in the breadcrumbs, parsley and reserved chicken and cook for *2–3 minutes* to heat the chicken through. If you feel the heat is too fierce, it may be lowered but the food should fry, not braise or boil.

3 Arrange a bed of red and yellow peppers dressed with the vinaigrette on 4 warmed serving plates. Transfer the chicken to the plates and serve, topped with the sautéed mushrooms.

Serves 4

Duck with Orange and Bean Sprouts

Preparation time: 10 minutes
Cooking time: 10–12 minutes

- pared rind of ½ orange
- 1 tablespoon cornflour
- 6 tablespoons water
- 1 tablespoon dry sherry or
  sherry vinegar
- 1 tablespoon orange juice
- 1 tablespoon soy sauce
- 2 teaspoons hoisin sauce
- 1 teaspoon soft dark brown
  sugar
- seeds of 6 cardamom pods,
  crushed
- 2 tablespoons groundnut or
  vegetable oil

- 1 garlic clove, crushed
- 2.5 cm/1 inch piece of fresh
  root ginger, peeled and cut
  into thin strips
- 375 g/12 oz duckling breast
  fillets, skin and fat removed,
  cut into strips crossways
- 250 g/8 oz bean sprouts
- 1 orange, peeled and
  segmented
- 1 bunch of spring onions,
  sliced (optional)

1 Cut the orange rind into matchstick strips, blanch in boiling water for *1 minute*, then drain, rinse and pat dry. Set aside.

2 Blend the cornflour in a jug with 2 tablespoons of the water, then add the remaining water, the sherry or vinegar, orange juice, soy and hoisin sauces, sugar and cardamom seeds. Stir well to combine.

3 Heat a wok or large frying pan until hot. Add the oil and heat over a moderate heat until hot. Add the garlic and ginger and stir-fry for a few seconds. Add the duckling, increase the heat to high and stir-fry for *3–4 minutes*. Pour in the cornflour mixture and bring to the boil over a high heat, stirring constantly until thickened and glossy. Stir-fry for *3 more minutes*, then add the bean sprouts and reserved orange rind and stir-fry for *1 minute* or until the duckling is tender. Add the orange segments and spring onions, if using, and heat through for *30 seconds*. Serve at once.

Serves 2–3

Turkey Escalopes with Wholegrain Mustard

Preparation time: 5 minutes
Cooking time: 12 minutes

- 15 g/½ oz butter
- 1 tablespoon sunflower oil
- 4 turkey escalopes, about
  75 g/3 oz each
- 150 ml/¼ pint chicken stock
- 6 tablespoons medium dry
  white wine
- 4 tablespoons wholegrain
  mustard (such as Meaux)
- 2 tablespoons double cream
  or Greek yogurt
- salt and pepper
- flat leaf parsley sprigs,
  to garnish

1 Melt the butter in the oil in a large saucepan over a moderate heat. Add the turkey escalopes and cook for *3 minutes* on each side. Season lightly then, using a slotted spoon, transfer to a serving dish and keep warm.

2 Add the stock and wine to the pan and bring to the boil, scraping up all the juices from the pan. Boil for *1 minute*.

3 In a cup, thin the mustard with 3 tablespoons of the pan liquid and stir back into the pan. Stirring constantly, cook for *1 minute*. Stir in the cream or yogurt and heat through gently without boiling.

4 Pour the sauce over the escalopes, garnish with the parsley and serve with thinly sliced, sautéed new potatoes and steamed sliced courgettes.

Serves 4

variation _____

Turkey Escalopes with Ginger Wine

Preparation time: 5 minutes
Cooking time: 12 minutes

- 25 g/1 oz butter
- 1 tablespoon sunflower oil
- 4 turkey escalopes, about
  75 g/3 oz each
- 6 tablespoons ginger wine
- 2 tablespoons orange juice
- 4 tablespoons double cream
- salt and pepper
- TO GARNISH:
- tarragon leaves
- orange slices, quartered

1 Follow step 1 of the main recipe using just half of the butter.

2 Add the remaining butter to the pan and melt over a medium heat. Add the ginger wine and orange juice and bring to the boil, scraping up all the juices from the pan. Boil for *1 minute*. Add the cream and stir over a medium heat until the sauce begins to bubble.

3 Pour the sauce over the escalopes, garnish with tarragon leaves and quartered orange slices and serve.

Serves 4

Creamy Thai-Style Prawn and Fish Curry

Preparation time: 15 minutes
Cooking time: 10 minutes

- 500 g/1 lb raw prawns
- 2 tablespoons peanut oil
- 500 g/1 lb thick fish fillets, cut into large cubes
- 1 tablespoon chopped fresh root ginger
- 1 tablespoon chopped lemon grass
- 1 tablespoon chopped fresh coriander stalk
- 1 tablespoon green curry powder or paste
- 1 teaspoon ground turmeric
- 300 ml/½ pint coconut cream
- 2 teaspoons grated lime rind
- 1 tablespoon lime juice
- 1 tablespoon fish sauce (nam pla)
- 3 spring onions, chopped
- fresh coriander, to garnish

1 Peel the prawns, leaving the tail and last section of shell of each prawn intact. Cut deeply down the centre back and remove the vein.

2 Heat half of the oil in a wok or large, heavy-based pan. Fry the prawns, then the fish, in small batches for *1 minute* or until the colour changes. Remove from the pan and set aside.

3 Heat the remaining oil in the pan. Add the ginger, lemon grass, coriander stalk, curry powder or paste and turmeric. Cook for *1 minute* or until the fragrance is released.

4 Add the coconut cream, lime rind and juice. Stir to combine and simmer for *1 minute*. Add the fish sauce, spring onions, the fish and the prawns. Cook for a further *1 minute*. Serve the curry at once, garnished with coriander.

Serves 6

Prawns with Vermicelli

Preparation time: 15 minutes
Cooking time: 15 minutes

- 125 g/4 oz belly of pork or
  6 rashers of rindless streaky
  bacon, sliced
- 3 tablespoons chopped fresh
  coriander, plus extra to
  garnish
- 3 garlic cloves, crushed
- 5 cm/2 inch piece of fresh
  root ginger, crushed
- 1 tablespoon whole black
  peppercorns

- 125 g/4 oz vermicelli, soaked
  in boiling water until soft
- 2 red chillies, finely sliced
- 8 raw king prawns, peeled
  and deveined (see opposite)
- 1 tablespoon oyster sauce
- 250 ml/8 fl oz chicken stock

1 Line the bottom of a flameproof casserole with the pork or bacon. Scatter the coriander, garlic, ginger and peppercorns over the meat, then add a layer of vermicelli and red chillies.

2 Arrange the prawns on top of the vermicelli, sprinkling them with oyster sauce. Pour in the stock, taking care not to disturb the prawns, cover tightly and cook over a high heat for *15 minutes*. Garnish with chopped coriander and serve immediately.

Serves 4

Roast Cod with Vegetables

Preparation time: 5 minutes
Cooking time: 25 minutes
Oven temperature: 230°C (450°F), Gas Mark 8

- 750 g/1½ lb cod fillets, skinned
- 4 potatoes, unpeeled and quartered
- 6 tomatoes, halved
- 1 red onion, quartered
- 1 fennel head, cut into wedges
- 2 garlic cloves, crushed
- 75 g/3 oz black olives, pitted
- 25 g/1 oz capers
- 4 tablespoons lemon juice
- 3 tablespoons olive oil
- salt and pepper
- handful of flat leaf parsley, chopped, to garnish

1 Put the cod, potatoes, tomatoes, onion and fennel into a large lightly oiled ovenproof dish. Try and arrange them in a single layer. Cover with the crushed garlic, olives, capers and lemon juice and season with salt and pepper. Drizzle with the olive oil and place in the top of a preheated oven, 230°C (450°F), Gas Mark 8, and roast for *25 minutes*.

2 Divide between 4 serving plates. Serve garnished with flat leaf parsley.

Serves 4

Pan-Fried Squid with Chillies

Preparation time: 10 minutes, plus marinating
Cooking time: 5 minutes

- 1 kg/2 lb ready prepared
  small squid
- 2 tablespoons olive oil
- 3 garlic cloves, crushed
- 1 red chilli, finely chopped

- 4 tablespoons lemon juice
- 2 tablespoons vegetable oil
- handful of flat leaf parsley,
  chopped

1 Slit the squid down one side and lay them flat. Score the skin of each one with a fine criss-cross pattern.

2 Mix the olive oil, garlic, chilli and lemon juice in a bowl and add the squid. Mix well to coat the squid all over, cover and marinate for *15 minutes*.

3 Remove the squid from the marinade, reserving the marinade. Heat a wok or large frying pan with the vegetable oil. Add the squid, stir well and cook over a high heat for *2–3 minutes*. The squid will curl up, but just hold them flat for a few seconds to brown the outside surface. Finally, add the strained marinade and the parsley to the pan, mix well and serve at once.

Serves 4

Wild Mushrooms in Crispy Bread Cases

Preparation time: 15 minutes
Cooking time: 10–15 minutes
Oven temperature: 200°C (400°F), Gas Mark 6

- assorted salad leaves, to serve

BREAD CASES:
- 8 thin slices of bread, crusts removed
- 50 g/2 oz butter, melted

FILLING:
- 25 g/1 oz butter
- 1 shallot, chopped

- 175 g/6 oz mushrooms (chestnut, oyster, shiitake), sliced
- 1 tablespoon Madeira
- 4 tablespoons double cream
- 1 tablespoon chopped flat leaf parsley
- salt and pepper

1 For the bread cases, brush both sides of the bread with the butter. Press firmly into 8 tartlet or bun tins. Bake the cases in a preheated oven, 200°C (400°F), Gas Mark 6, for *10–15* minutes, until crisp and golden brown.

2 Meanwhile, make the filling. Melt the butter in a small saucepan, add the shallot and fry for about *5 minutes*, until softened. Add the mushrooms and cook for a further *5 minutes*, until tender. Stir in the Madeira and allow to bubble briefly, then stir in the cream and chopped parsley, with salt and pepper to taste. Cook over a medium heat for a few minutes, until the mixture forms a sauce.

3 Arrange the salad leaves on 8 small plates and place a bread case on each one. Fill the bread cases with the mushroom mixture and serve warm.

Serves 8

variation _____

Chicken, Celery and Bacon Tartlets

Preparation time: 15 minutes
Cooking time: 10–15 minutes
Oven temperature: 200°C (400°F), Gas Mark 6

- 8 bread cases, see main recipe
- assorted salad leaves, to serve

FILLING:
- 25 g/1 oz butter
- 1 celery stick, sliced
- 2 rashers of rindless smoked back bacon, chopped

- 125 g/4 oz boneless, skinless chicken breasts, chopped
- 1 tablespoon sherry
- 3 tablespoons double cream
- 1 tablespoon chopped flat leaf parsley
- salt and pepper

1 Prepare the bread cases and filling as in the main recipe, substituting celery for the shallot and using the bacon and chicken instead of the mushrooms. Use the sherry in place of the Madeira and finish as in the main recipe.

In the Store Cupboard

A sensibly stocked store cupboard invariably results in effortless cooking, and there are many more useful items besides those shown here. For example, there are plenty more types of pasta, noodles and rice worth keeping handy. Consider various canned foods; dried mushrooms; packet croûtons for soups and salads; assorted oriental sauces and of course a whole host of spices and dried herbs among others.

Olive oil

Cardamoms

Sun-dried tomatoes

Black peppercorns

Balsamic vinegar

Pesto

Olive oil varies in depth of colour and flavour according to its quality. It is used in salads and cooking.

Black peppercorns are the sun-dried shrivelled berries of the pepper vine, *Piper nigrum*.

Cardamoms are green or black aromatic pods, which if used whole must be removed from food before serving.

Balsamic vinegar is a well-matured Italian vinegar with a rich, aromatic, sweet taste. It

is used in dressings, sauces and marinades.

Sun-dried tomatoes have a concentrated flavour and are sold in jars in olive oil or loose, as here, when they need soaking in water before use.

Pesto is a strongly flavoured sauce made from fresh basil, pine nuts, garlic and hard cheese. Available in small jars, it is ideal with pasta.

Olives may be cured in brine, packed in oil or flavoured with herbs or garlic. The difference in colour relates to the degree of ripeness.

Dried chillies are very powerful and should be used sparingly. As with fresh chillies, they need careful handling – keep them away from your eyes and face.

Sesame oil is an essential ingredient in oriental cooking, usually used in the final minutes of stir-frying, or in salad dressings or marinades.

Dried pasta comes in a variety of shapes and sizes: tagliatelle is flat and ribbon - like; macaroni is tubular and linguine is a string-like pasta.

Egg noodles are sold in compressed bundles of various sizes, and usually require little cooking.

Chilli sauce is used worldwide to add heat and flavour to food. It can be thick or thin, and ranges from dark brown to bright red.

Dried chillies

Chilli sauce

Tagliatelle

Sesame oil

Egg noodles

Olives

Macaroni

Linguine

Salmon Fillets with Spanish Salsa

Preparation time: 17 minutes, plus 5 minutes standing
Cooking time: 8 minutes

- 2 teaspoons finely grated lime rind
- 5 tablespoons lime juice
- 5 tablespoons olive oil
- 1 small red onion, finely chopped
- 4 small tomatoes, skinned and finely chopped
- handful of mint leaves
- 2 limes, flesh only, finely chopped

- 2 tablespoons white wine vinegar
- 2 teaspoons sugar
- few drops of Tabasco sauce
- 3 slices of lemon
- splash of white wine (optional)
- 4 salmon fillets
- 125 g/4 oz roasted, salted peanuts, to garnish

1 Combine the lime rind and juice, olive oil, red onion, tomatoes, mint, lime flesh, vinegar, sugar and Tabasco and stand for *5 minutes*.

2 Fill a deep wide pan two-thirds full with water. Add the lemon slices and white wine, if using. Bring to the boil. Reduce the heat and simmer. Carefully put the salmon fillets into the pan and cook in the simmering liquid for about *6 minutes*, depending on their thickness.

3 Using a fish slice, transfer the fish from the pan to individual plates. Top the fish with the tomato mixture and sprinkle with roasted, salted peanuts. Serve at once with a mixed salad and some lime wedges if liked.

Serves 4

Sesame Lamb Salad

Preparation time: 20 minutes
Cooking time: 10 minutes

- 875 g/1¾ lb lamb fillet, cut into 2 pieces
- 2 tablespoons oil
- 1 large carrot, cut into 5 cm/ 2 inch lengths then into thin strips
- 1 large courgette, cut into 5 cm/2 inch lengths then into thin strips
- 150 g/5 oz mangetout, thinly sliced
- 24 spinach leaves
- pepper

DRESSING:

- 5 tablespoons oil
- ¼ teaspoon sesame oil
- 2 tablespoons soy sauce
- 2 tablespoons sherry
- 1 garlic clove, crushed
- 1 teaspoon soft brown sugar
- 1 tablespoon toasted sesame seeds

1 Trim the lamb of any excess fat and sinew. Rub each piece with a little oil and season with pepper. Heat the remaining oil in a heavy-based frying pan. Sear each side of the fillets over a high heat. Cook, turning often, for a further *6–8 minutes*. Allow the fillets to stand for *10 minutes*, then cut 12 slices across the grain, each about 2.5 cm/1 inch thick .

2 Combine the carrot, courgette and mangetout. Arrange the spinach leaves on a serving platter. Top with the vegetables and lamb fillets.

3 To make the dressing, combine all the ingredients in a small, screw-top jar. Shake vigorously until the ingredients are well combined. Drizzle the dressing over the salad just before serving.

Serves 6

Pan-cooked Rabbit with Sage

Preparation time: 5 minutes
Cooking time: 25 minutes

- 2 tablespoons olive oil
- 1 rabbit, cut into 8 pieces
- handful of chopped sage
- rosemary sprigs
- 150 ml/¼ pint dry white wine
- 1 tablespoon Dijon mustard

- salt and pepper

TO SERVE:

- 375 g/12 oz three-colour
  pappardelle
- handful of chopped flat leaf
  parsley, to garnish

1 Heat the oil in a large frying pan, add the rabbit pieces and brown all over. Season well with salt and pepper. Add the sage, rosemary, wine and mustard; mix thoroughly and coat the rabbit in the wine sauce.

2 Simmer the rabbit for *20 minutes* over a gentle heat, turning it frequently so that it cooks evenly.

3 While the rabbit is cooking, place the pappardelle in a pan of salted boiling water and cook for 12–15 minutes, or according to packet instructions.

4 Divide the pasta between 4 plates and place 2 pieces of rabbit on each plate. Spoon over the sauce and serve garnished with the chopped parsley.

Serves 4

Avocado and Mushroom Salad

Preparation time: 15 minutes

- 25 g/1 oz pine nuts
- 250 g/8 oz button
  mushrooms, quartered
- ½ head of curly endive
- 1 lime or small lemon
- 3 avocados
- grated rind of ½ lemon

DRESSING:

- 6 tablespoons olive oil
- 3–4 tablespoons lime juice
- 1 garlic clove, crushed
- 1 teaspoon crushed
  coriander seeds
- 1 teaspoon honey
- salt and pepper

1 First toast the pine nuts under a grill for about 5 minutes or until brown, be careful not to burn them. Spread them on a heavy baking sheet and toast under a preheated hot grill, tossing frequently until an even, golden brown colour. (Take care not to over brown them or they will taste bitter.) Set aside to cool.

2 Mix together the dressing ingredients and season to taste with salt and pepper. Put the mushrooms in a large bowl, pour over the dressing and toss well, until all the mushrooms are coated.

3 Arrange the endive in a serving bowl. Squeeze the juice from half the lime or lemon; slice the remainder. Halve the avocados, remove and discard the stones. Slice the avocados, sprinkle with lime or lemon juice to prevent discoloration and arrange on top of the endive. Spoon the mushrooms into the centre. Sprinkle over the toasted pine nuts and lemon rind and garnish with the lime or lemon slices. Serve immediately.

Serves 4

Desserts

Something sweet invariably goes down well at the end of a meal. It could be the light, simple option of seasonal fresh fruit served with thick crème fraîche or Greek yogurt, or a more elaborate chocolate favourite. Whatever you choose, all of the recipes here demonstrate just how little time it can take to create a delightful sweet sensation.

Mango Puff Tartlets

Preparation time: 10 minutes
Cooking time: 12–15 minutes
Oven temperature: 220°C (425°F), Gas Mark 7

- 250 g/8 oz puff pastry,
  thawed if frozen
- 1 ripe mango
- 25 g/1 oz unsalted butter
- 4 teaspoons caster sugar
- 2 tablespoons apricot jam

1 Divide the puff pastry into quarters. Roll out each piece to a 10 cm/4 inch round. Space out the pastry rounds on a greased baking sheet.

2 Peel the mango and cut it in half around the stone. Cut each half in half again. Slice the mango quarters thinly and arrange over the pastry rounds.

3 Dot some butter over each mango and sprinkle with the caster sugar. Bake in a preheated oven, 220°C (425°F), Gas Mark 7, for *12–15 minutes*, until the pastry is risen and golden and the mango is tender.

4 Warm the apricot jam in a small saucepan, press it through a sieve into a bowl, then carefully brush over the top of each mango tartlet. Serve the tartlets warm.

Serves 4

variations

Peach Puff Tartlets

Replace the mango with 4 peach halves, skinned, thinly sliced and arranged as in the main recipe.

Pear Puff Tartlets

Replace the mango with 2 ripe pears, peeled, cored and halved, then sliced and arranged as in the main recipe.

Apple Puff Tartlets

Replace the mango with 2 eating apples, peeled, cored and halved, then thinly sliced and arranged as in the main recipe. Sprinkle 1 tablespoon flaked almonds over the tartlets before baking.

Alaska Crumble Pie

Preparation time: 15 minutes, plus chilling
Cooking time: 5–8 minutes
Oven temperature: 200°C (400°F), Gas Mark 6

- 175 g/6 oz oat biscuits
- 75 g/3 oz butter

FILLING:

- 3 egg whites
- 175 g/6 oz caster sugar

- 125 g/4 oz raspberries
- 125 g/4 oz redcurrants
- 500 ml/17 fl oz vanilla
  ice cream

1 For the crumb base, crush the biscuits in a food processor. Alternatively, place them between 2 sheets of greaseproof paper and crush with a rolling pin. Melt the butter in a pan, add the crumbs and stir well. Press the mixture evenly over the base and sides of a 23 cm/9 inch pie plate or flan tin and chill until ready to serve.

2 Whisk the egg whites in a grease-free bowl until they are stiff and dry. Gently whisk in 1 tablespoon of the sugar, then fold in the remainder.

3 When ready to serve, fill the crumb case with the fruit and add scoops of ice cream. Spread the meringue over the top, covering the filling completely. Bake in a preheated oven, 200°C (400°F), Gas Mark 6, for *5–8 minutes*, until the meringue is golden. Serve immediately.

Serves 4–6

Chocolate Swirl Tart

Make this delicious tart in minutes, and then you can simply leave it to chill to perfection.

Preparation time: 20 minutes, plus chilling

- 125 g/4 oz digestive biscuits
- 50 g/2 oz amaretti biscuits
- 75 g/3 oz butter

FILLING:

- 200 g/7 oz dark chocolate
- 300 ml/½ pint double cream

1 Crush the biscuits in a food processor. Alternatively, place them between 2 sheets of greaseproof paper and crush with a rolling pin. Melt the butter in a saucepan and stir in the crumbs. Press the mixture into a greased 23 cm/9 inch pie plate or flan tin. Chill in the refrigerator until firm.

2 Break up the chocolate and place in a heatproof bowl over a pan of hot, not boiling, water. Stir gently until the chocolate has melted. Cover a rolling pin with foil and brush lightly with oil. Drizzle a little of the melted chocolate from the tip of a teaspoon or a small piping bag on to the rolling pin in zig-zag lines about 2.5 cm/1 inch long. Chill until set.

3 Whip the double cream until stiff and fold into the remaining melted chocolate. Do not over fold as you want a swirled effect. Spoon into the chilled crumb case and chill for about *2 hours*, until set.

4 Just before serving, carefully peel the chocolate decorations from the foil and pile into the centre of the tart.

Serves 6–8

Chocolate Crumb Tart with Exotic Fruit

Another luscious tart to make quickly in advance
and leave to chill until you're ready to serve.

Preparation time: 20 minutes, plus chilling

CRUMB CASE:

- 175 g/6 oz chocolate
  digestive biscuits
- 75 g/3 oz butter
- 1 tablespoon golden syrup

FILLING:

- 300 ml/½ pint crème fraîche
- selection of exotic fruit (such
  as papaya, pineapple, cape
  gooseberries, pomegranate,
  star fruit, kumquat), sliced
- 2 tablespoons redcurrant
  jelly
- 1 tablespoon lime juice

1 For the crumb base, crush the biscuits in a food processor.
Alternatively, place them between 2 sheets of greaseproof
paper and crush with a rolling pin. Melt the butter with the
syrup in a saucepan. Stir in the crumbs. Press the mixture on
to the base and sides of a greased, deep 20 cm/8 inch pie
plate or flan tin and chill until firm.

2 Remove the crumb case from the pie plate or flan tin and
place on a serving plate.

3 Fill the crumb case with crème fraîche and arrange the fruit
over the top. Warm the redcurrant jelly with the lime juice in a
small saucepan and drizzle over the fruit. Chill the tart for up to
2 hours until ready to serve.

Serves 6

variation _____

... with Crystallized Fruit

Preparation time: 20 minutes

- 1 chocolate crumb case, see
  main recipe

FILLING:

- 250 g/8 oz cream cheese,
  softened
- 75 g/3 oz caster sugar

- 1 teaspoon grated lemon
  rind
- 4 tablespoons single cream
- 175 g/6 oz mixed crystallized
  fruit, thinly sliced

1 For the filling, beat together the cream cheese, caster
sugar, lemon rind and cream in a bowl. Fill the biscuit crumb
case with the cream cheese mixture, smoothing the top.

2 Arrange the crystallized fruit attractively on top and serve
the flan cold.

Serves 6

Peaches with Almond Filling

Preparation time: 10 minutes
Cooking time: 15 minutes
Oven temperature: 180°C (350°F), Gas Mark 4

- 125 g/4 oz golden syrup
- 25 g/1 oz butter, chopped
- 4 large, firm ripe peaches, halved and pitted
- 125g/4 oz amaretti biscuits, crushed

- 175g/6 oz unblanched almonds, chopped
- 20 g/¾ oz grated or desiccated coconut
- 75 ml/3 fl oz orange juice
- 2 tablespoons brown sugar

1 Put the golden syrup and butter into a large ovenproof dish. Add the peaches, skin side down. Cover and cook in a preheated oven, 180°C (350°F), Gas Mark 4, for *8–10 minutes*.

2 Place the biscuits, almonds and coconut in a mixing bowl and stir to combine. Add the orange juice and mix gently until all of the mixture is moistened.

3 Spoon the mixture evenly on to each peach half and sprinkle with the brown sugar. Return the peaches to the oven and cook, uncovered, for *5 minutes*. Spoon the syrup from the baking dish over the peaches when serving.

Serves 8

Blueberry Crème Brûlée

Preparation time: 10 minutes, plus 15 minutes freezing
Cooking time: 4 minutes

- oil or melted butter, for greasing
- 300 g/10 oz blueberries or raspberries, or a mixture of both
- 250 ml/8 fl oz thick Greek yogurt

- 500 ml/17 fl oz good-quality vanilla ice cream, softened at room temperature for 15–20 minutes before using
- 75 g/3 oz soft brown sugar
- crisp, sweet dessert biscuits, to serve

1 Brush six 125 ml/4 fl oz freezerproof ramekin dishes with oil or melted butter. Divide the fruit evenly between each dish.

2 Combine the Greek yogurt and softened ice cream in a bowl, and whisk to mix thoroughly. Spoon the mixture evenly over the fruit. Place the ramekins in the freezer for at least *15 minutes* before serving.

3 Just before serving, sprinkle each ramekin with 2 table-spoons of the soft brown sugar, then toast under a preheated hot grill for about *4 minutes* until the sugar melts. Serve with dessert biscuits.

Serves 6

Pineapple with Rum

Preparation time: 2 minutes
Cooking time: 15 minutes

- 90 g/3½ oz caster sugar
- grated rind and juice of
  1 orange
- 2 tablespoons lemon juice

- 40 g/1½ oz unsalted butter
- 4 thick slices of pineapple
- 2 tablespoons Kirsch or rum

1 Put the sugar, grated rind and juices in a frying pan. Bring to the boil slowly, stirring until the sugar dissolves and the mixture thickens to a syrup.

2 Lower the heat and add the unsalted butter. Swirl it around the pan until melted.

3 Add the pineapple slices and cook them gently for about *10 minutes* until heated through, turning them once, and basting them regularly with the syrup. Remove the pan from the heat and lift each pineapple slice out of the pan separately with a slotted spoon. Place them in warmed individual serving dishes.

4 Pour the Kirsch or rum into the pan. Carefully set the syrup alight and pour it, still flaming, over the pineapple slices. Serve at once.

Serves 4

variation

Bananas with Rum

Preparation time: 2 minutes
Cooking time: 4 minutes

- 25 g/1 oz unsalted butter
- 25 g/1 oz soft brown sugar

- 4 bananas, halved
  lengthways
- 2 tablespoons rum

1 Heat the butter in a frying pan until melted then stir in the soft brown sugar. Add the bananas to the pan and cook gently for *3 minutes*, turning once.

2 Arrange the bananas on warmed serving dishes and spoon over the juices.

3 Warm the rum in a ladle, ignite and pour over the bananas. Serve flaming, with cream.

Serves 4

Raspberry Meringue Soufflé

Preparation time: 20 minutes
Cooking time: 1–2 minutes

- 400 g/13 oz raspberries
- 125 g/4 oz caster sugar
- 5 egg whites
- 2 tablespoons icing sugar

1 Divide half of the fresh raspberries evenly over the bases of six soufflé dishes, 125 ml/4 fl oz capacity. Place the remaining raspberries and half of the caster sugar in a liquidizer or food processor. Blend for *1 minute* or until the mixture is smooth.

2 Place the egg whites into a large dry mixing bowl. Whisk the egg whites until firm peaks form. Gradually add the remaining caster sugar, beating well between each addition. Beat until all the sugar dissolves.

3 Using a large metal spoon, gently fold the raspberry purée into the egg whites. Spoon the mixture evenly into each soufflé dish to about 3 cm/1¼ inches above the rim.

4 Place the soufflés on a baking sheet and cook under a preheated medium grill for *1 minute* or so, or until the tops are golden brown. Dust with icing sugar and serve at once.

Serves 6

Grilled Apple Stack

Preparation time: 10 minutes
Cooking time: 10 minutes

- 4 large green apples
- butter, to taste
- lime marmalade

- cream, ice cream or custard, to serve

1 Cut the apples into thin slices and place on a lightly greased, cold grill pan. Top each slice with a small knob of butter and ½ teaspoon of lime marmalade. Cook under a preheated hot grill until the butter is melted and the apple is golden brown.

2 Serve 4–5 apple slices stacked on top of one another (make sure that the apple slices are cool enough to handle) with a spoonful of cream, ice cream or custard.

Serves 4

Oranges in Caramel

Preparation time: 10–15 minutes, plus chilling
Cooking time: 10 minutes

- 8 small oranges
- 250 g/8 oz sugar
- 125 ml/4 fl oz cold water
- 150 ml/¼ pint hot water
- brandy snaps, to serve

1 Pare the rind from 1 orange and shred finely. Cook the rind in boiling water for *1 minute*, then drain and dry.

2 Peel the oranges, removing all the pith. Cut into thin slices and arrange on a serving dish in the shape of oranges.

3 Place the sugar and cold water in a pan. Heat gently until dissolved, then boil steadily to a rich brown caramel. Carefully add the hot water and stir until the caramel has melted, heating again if necessary. Leave to cool.

4 Pour the caramel over the oranges, top with the shredded rind and chill. Serve with brandy snaps.

Serves 4

Tropical Fruit Salad with Mango Cream

Preparation time: 10 minutes, plus chilling
Cooking time: 10 minutes

- 125 g/4 oz sugar
- 250 ml/8 fl oz water
- 1 lemon, sliced
- grated rind of 1 orange
- 425 g/14 oz can pineapple pieces
- 3 peaches, sliced
- 3 kiwi fruit, peeled and quartered
- 250 g/8 oz strawberries, halved
- 2 bananas, sliced

MANGO CREAM:
- 2 ripe mangoes, peeled and stoned
- 50 g/2 oz brown sugar
- 250 ml/8 fl oz low-fat soured cream
- ¼ teaspoon ground cardamom

1 For the mango cream, place the mangoes, brown sugar, soured cream and cardamom into a food processor or blender and blend until smooth. Refrigerate until required.

2 Place the sugar, water, sliced lemon and orange rind in a saucepan. Stir over a low heat until the sugar dissolves. Simmer for *5 minutes*, then add the undrained pineapple.

3 Place the peaches, kiwi fruit, strawberries and bananas in a serving dish. Pour the pineapple mixture over. Refrigerate until required.

4 Serve the fruit salad in individual bowls with the mango cream served separately.

Serves 6

Melon and Raspberries

This simple but very delicious dessert originates from the south of France, where small melons and raspberries are plentiful in the summer.

Preparation time: 15 minutes, plus chilling

- 2 or 3 small melons
- 250 g/8 oz raspberries
- 75 g/3 oz cream cheese
- 150 ml/¼ pint crème fraîche
- 50 g/2 oz caster sugar
- 1–2 tablespoons Curaçao,
  brandy or sweet sherry

TO DECORATE:
- 50 g/2 oz raspberries
- caster sugar
- mint or raspberry leaves

1 Halve the melons and scoop out the seeds. Chill while you prepare the raspberry filling.

2 Crush or sieve the raspberries, blend with the cream cheese, then gradually whip in the crème fraîche. Add the sugar and the alcohol.

3 Chill, or freeze very slightly until just before serving, then spoon into the melon halves. Decorate with whole raspberries, caster sugar and mint or raspberry leaves.

Serves 4–6

variation _____
Melon and Plums

Preparation time: 5 minutes, plus chilling

- 2 or 3 prepared small
  melons, see main recipe
- 500 g/1 lb ripe plums, pitted
  and sliced
- 425 g/14 oz can black
  cherries, drained and pitted
- 200 ml/7 fl oz crème fraîche
- mint leaves, to decorate

1 Place the plums and cherries in a bowl and mix lightly. Spoon into the melon halves and top each with crème fraîche. Decorate with mint leaves and serve.

Serves 4–6

makes 2 litres/3¹/2 pints

1.5 litres/2³/4 pints red grape juice

300 ml/10 fl oz orange juice

75 ml/2¹/2 fl oz cranberry juice

50 ml/1³/4 fl oz lemon juice

50 ml/1³/4 fl oz lime juice

100 ml/3¹/2 fl oz sugar syrup

ice cubes

to decorate

slices of lemon

slices of orange

slices of lime

soft sangria

Put the grape juice, orange juice, cranberry juice, lemon juice, lime juice and sugar syrup into a chilled punch bowl and stir well.

Add the ice and decorate with the slices of lemon, orange and lime.

Recipe Photographers:
Reed Consumer Books
  Ltd./Nick Carman
/David Loftus
/James Murphy
/Peter Myers /Roger Stowell

Special Photography:
Philip Webb
Home Economist:
Sarah Ramsbottom
Jacket Photographer:
Peter Myers / Sean Myers
Jacket Home Economist:
Sunil Vijayakar